MAMM!OTHS

ASHLEY GISH

ICE AGE CREATURES X BOOKS

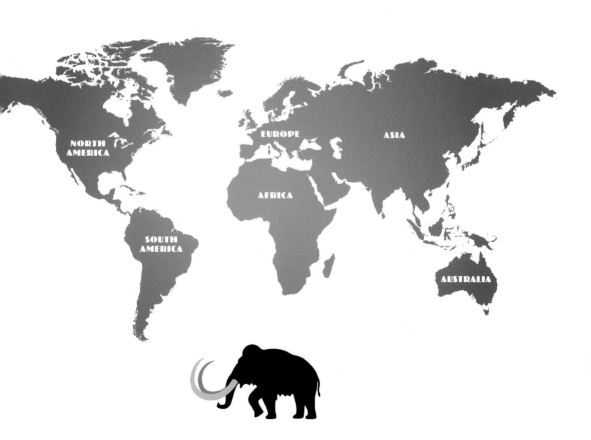

NORTH AMERICA

EUROPE

ASIA

AFRICA

SOUTH AMERICA

AUSTRALIA

CREATIVE EDUCATION · CREATIVE PAPERBACKS

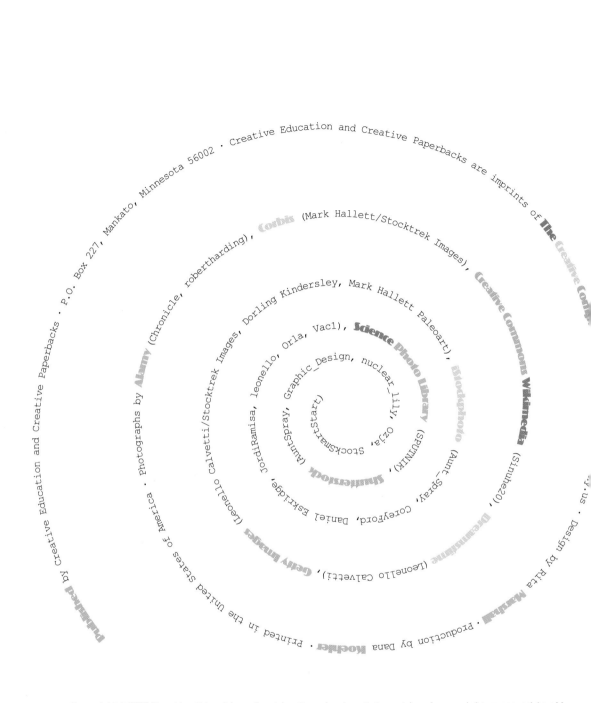

Published by Creative Education and Creative Paperbacks · P.O. Box 227, Mankato, Minnesota 56002 · Creative Education and Creative Paperbacks are imprints of The Creative Company · www.thecreativecompany.us · Design by Rita Marshall · Production by Dana Kodsha · Printed in the United States of America · Photographs by Alamy (Chronicle, robertharding), Corbis (Mark Hallett/Stocktrek Images), Creative Commons Wikimedia (Sinhez20), Dreamstime, Getty Images (Leonello Calvetti), iStockphoto (JordiRamisa, leonello, Orla, Vac1), Science Photo Library (Mark Hallett Paleoart), Shutterstock (Aunt_Spray, Coreyford, Daniel Eskridge, Graphic_Design, nuclear_lily, Orla, SPUTNIK), StockSmartStart

Library of Congress Cataloging-in-Publication Data · Names: Gish, Ashley, author. · Title: Mammoths / by Ashley Gish. · Description: Mankato, Minnesota: The Creative Company, [2023] · Series: X-books: ice age creatures · Includes bibliographical references and index. · Audience: Ages 6–8 | Grades 2–3 · Summary: "A countdown of five of the most captivating mammoth fossil discoveries and relatives provides thrills as readers discover more about the biological, social, and hunting characteristics of these Ice Age creatures"—Provided by publisher. · Identifiers: LCCN 2021044418 | ISBN 9781640264359 (library binding) | ISBN 9781628329681 (paperback) | ISBN 9781640006096 (ebook) · Subjects: LCSH: Mammoths—Juvenile literature. · Classification: LCC QE882.P8 G57 2023 · DDC 569/.67—dc23/eng/20211116 · LC record available at https://lccn.loc.gov/2021044418

MAMM!OTHS

CONTENTS

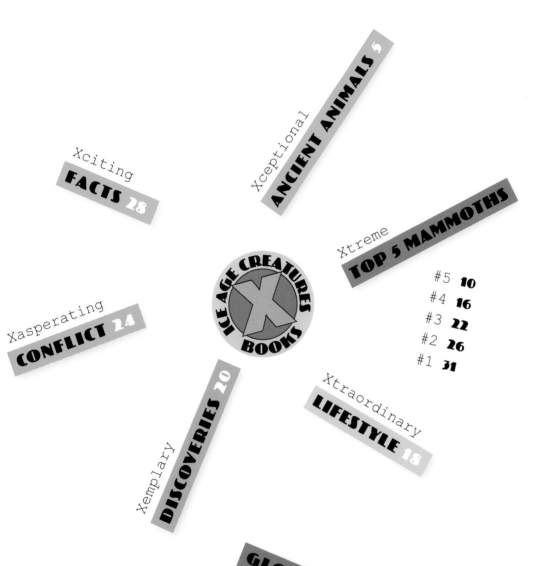

Xciting
FACTS 28

Xceptional
ANCIENT ANIMALS 5

Xtreme
TOP 5 MAMMOTHS

#5 **10**
#4 **16**
#3 **22**
#2 **26**
#1 **31**

Xasperating
CONFLICT 24

Xtraordinary
LIFESTYLE 18

Xemplary
DISCOVERIES 20

GLOSSARY

RESOURCES

INDEX 32

ICE AGE CREATURES
BOOKS

XCEPTIONAL ANCIENT ANIMALS

Huge mammoths lived during the Ice Age. Some weighed as much as two African elephants combined! Mammoths roamed from Siberia to North America.

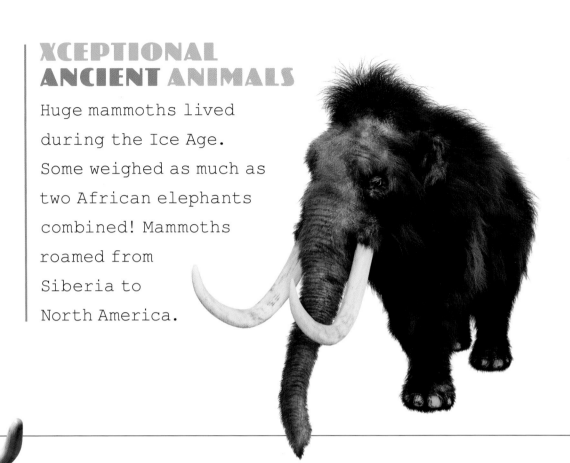

Mammoth Basics

Mammoths were **mammals**. A long trunk hung from their flat faces. They used it to smell things and pick up food. They had two large teeth called tusks. One grew on either side of the trunk. Some mammoths' tusks grew up to 15 feet (4.6 m) long.

The mammoths we usually think of today are woolly mammoths. They lived from about 120,000 to 3,700 years ago. Their shaggy hair ranged in color from blonde to black. Under their skin, woolly mammoths had a four-inch (10.2-cm) layer of fat. It helped keep them warm on the cold **steppe**.

MAMMOTHS AROUND THE WORLD

= woolly mammoth range

NORTH AMERICA

COSTA RICA

WOOLLY MAMMOTHS

lived throughout Europe, northern Asia, and parts of North America.

COLUMBIAN MAMMOTHS

lived as far south as Costa Rica.

Adults ate nearly 400 pounds (181 kg) of food every day!

BIG EATERS

Columbian mammoths lived in southern North America. They were mostly hairless, like modern elephants.

Steppe mammoths were the biggest kind of mammoth. They weighed up to 31,000 pounds (14,061 kg)! They were nearly as tall as giraffes. Woolly mammoths weighed about 12,000 pounds (5,443 kg). That is similar to an African elephant.

GENTLE GIANTS

Mammoths ate grasses, mosses, and leafy plants.

MAMMOTH BASICS FACT

Mammoths would have drunk a lot of water every day.

Some mammoths became stuck in mud and died.

TOP FIVE XTREME MAMMOTHS

Xtreme Mammoth #5

Mammoth Mummy In 2007, some reindeer herders made an amazing discovery. They found a baby woolly mammoth in the frozen Siberian soil. She had died 41,800 years ago. But she looked like she had died recently. Researchers named her Lyuba, which means "love." They believe she became stuck in deep mud. Before her mother could pluck her out, the mud buried her. She was just the second **mummified** mammoth calf ever discovered.

Mammoth Beginnings

During an ice age, worldwide temperatures fall. Snow and ice cover large parts of the world. Much of the landscape is vast grasslands. Experts believe Earth has gone through five ice ages. The most recent one ended about 10,000 years ago. It is often called the Ice Age.

Many animals, like mammoths, grew large during the Ice Age. Some had thick fur. Woolly mammoths were equipped for living in cold weather. Even their blood contained substances that kept it from freezing quickly. Mammoths, rhinoceroses, sloths, and bison were plant-eaters. Big predators included saber-toothed cats, dire wolves, and cave bears.

1974

2003

Mammoth bones,
South Dakota

Mammoth tooth,
St. Paul Island, Alaska

2007

Mummified calf,
Siberia

2018

Flint tip of spear found stuck
in mammoth rib bone, Poland

MAMMOTH BEGINNINGS FACT

Columbian and woolly mammoths

were able to have babies with each other.

TOP FIVE XTREME MAMMOTHS

Xtreme Mammoth #4

Giants in the Land More than 1,000 years ago, people living on the island of Crete found huge skeletons. The skulls had large teeth and long tusks. Each skull had a big hole in the middle. It looked like an eye socket. The people put the bones together. The skeletons looked like giants with one eye and huge fangs! But the bones had been put together incorrectly. The remains were actually ancient mammoth relatives.

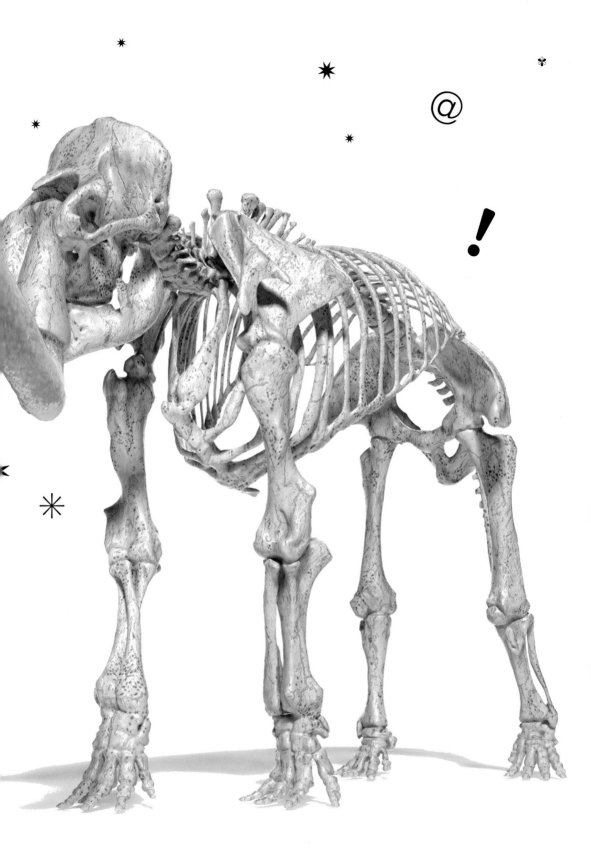

XTRAORDINARY LIFESTYLE

Mammoths and elephants share a common relative called *Primelephas*. They have a complex family tree. Mammoths look strange compared with animals living today.

Mammoth Society

Primelephas lived about 6 million years ago. It **evolved** and eventually gave rise to mammoths and elephants. Mammoths traveled in family groups, like elephants do. The groups were led by an older female.

Today, there are two kinds of elephants. African elephants are too wild to train. Asian elephants can be trained to work. Some Asian elephants carry supplies on their backs. They lift heavy objects with their trunks. Asian elephants are the closest living relatives of woolly mammoths. Other surprising relatives include manatees and hyraxes.

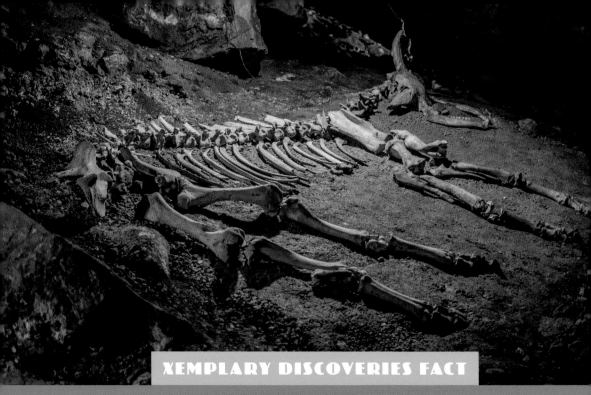

Sometimes scientists can figure out what

a mammoth ate for its last meal!

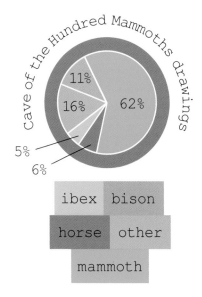

Cave of the Hundred Mammoths drawings

11%

16%

62%

5%

6%

ibex | bison

horse | other

mammoth

XEMPLARY DISCOVERIES

Some scientists study animals that have died out. They look at **fossils** and other animal remains. Many mummified mammoths have been found.

The cold places where mammoths lived preserved their bodies after they died. Some of these remains are made of soft tissue and blood. Researchers learn about an animal from its mummified body. They learn its weight and the color of its hair or fur.

Some of the most remarkable mammoth discoveries were created by early humans. Thousands of years ago, humans painted and carved on cave walls. They used art to tell stories. These were mainly stories about hunting. A cave in France is called the Cave of the Hundred Mammoths. Most of the animals pictured there are mammoths.

TOP FIVE XTREME MAMMOTHS

Xtreme Mammoth #3

Pygmy Mammoths Some of the smallest mammoths lived on an island between Siberia and Alaska. St. Paul Island was small and safe. Mammoths living there grew smaller over many decades. They shrank to the size of a modern horse. Changes in the Earth's temperature affected their water sources. Ponds and lakes dried up. These mammoths might have died of thirst.

XASPERATING CONFLICT

Changes in Earth's temperatures caused many animals to die out. Early humans hunted mammoths. This greatly reduced the animals' numbers.

Mammoth Survival

Mammoths and humans lived at the same time. Scientists also know humans hunted mammoths. In 2018, scientists examined a fossilized mammoth rib. It was 25,000 years old. A piece of flint spearhead was stuck in it. The spearhead could have come from only one source: human hunters!

Today, some people hunt elephants. This is illegal. These people are called poachers. They sell elephant tusks. Buyers use the tusks to make decorations. Poachers have killed many elephants.

The last mammoths lived on Wrangel Island in the Arctic Ocean. Rising seawater cut this area off from the mainland. New mammoths could not get there. Generations of mating with relatives caused the woolly mammoths to lose their sense of smell. Their hair was silky instead of woolly and warm. The small population could not recover. They died out around 4,000 years ago.

MAMMOTH SURVIVAL FACT

Flint is a type of stone humans used to make arrowheads and spearheads. Flint can be chipped into sharp edges and points.

TOP FIVE XTREME MAMMOTHS

Xtreme Mammoth #2

Mammoth Graveyard In 1974, George Hanson was leveling ground in Hot Springs, South Dakota. One day, he hit something in the dirt. It was a tusk. The tusk was seven feet (2.1 m) long! Hanson soon found other fossils. A team of professors and students came to the site. They uncovered many mammoth fossils. Today, the area is known as the Mammoth Site of Hot Springs, South Dakota.

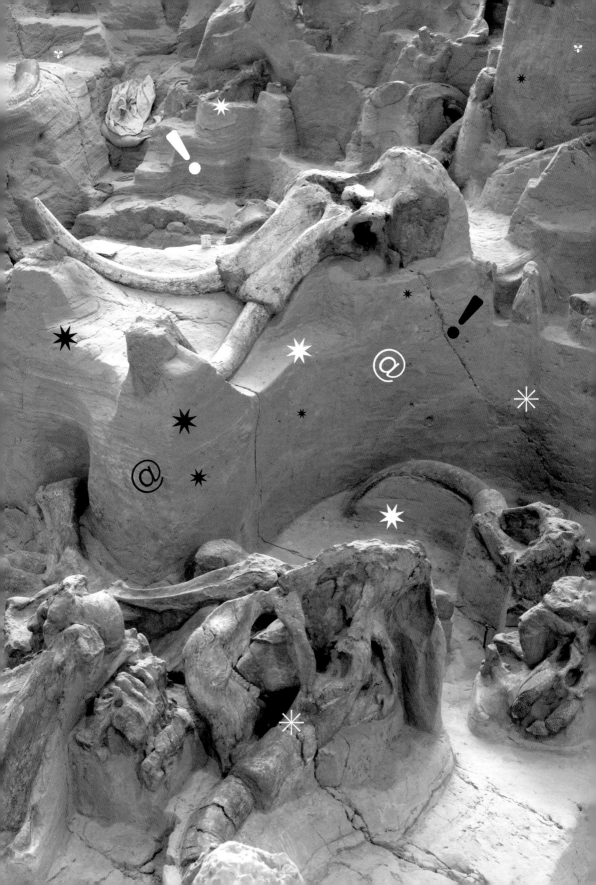

XCITING FACTS

Pygmy mammoths were rare. They lived on only one island in the worl

Mammoths were so big that most predators did not attack them. But young or sick mammoths were easy targets.

Early humans made spear shafts from mammoth tusks.

Scientists who study fossils often work with geologists. Geologists study rocks, minerals, and soil.

Mammoths came to North America from Asia. The continents were once connected by land.

Fossils do not contain blood or soft tissue, such as skin.

Early humans ate mammoths. Mammoth bones were used to make tools, weapons, and shelters.

In 2011, the leg bone of a dwarf mammoth was found on the island of Crete.

Mammoths used their long tail hairs to swat bothersome flies.

Mammoths' skulls have a big hole in the center where the trunk grew.

Mammoths used their tusks to dig in snow and soil, scrape tree bark, and fight predators and other mammoths.

Researchers think smaller, faster animals were better at escaping human hunters.

Mammoths probably lived to be about 60 years old.

Experts once believed humans hunted mammoths by

chasing them off cliffs. New studies show that humans used spears.